FLIP-FLOPS
Are *STILL* Not An Option!

*Essentials of Professional Conduct
for Catholic Educators*

D0901798

SAL GUCCIONE

2ND EDITION

NCEA®
National Catholic Educational Association

ISBN   978-1-55833-592-9
Part No. SDV-22-1550

Table of Contents

Introduction

> *"What the teacher is, is more important than what he teaches."*
> —Karl A. Menninger

Being a **Catholic School Teacher** is, without a doubt, a most rewarding and fulfilling career and life adventure. Whether you are a veteran teacher or beginning your very first year, you have been called to an important ministry of the Church. In a Catholic school you have many opportunities to lead and guide students academically, socially and spiritually. Through your positive example, you enable students to grow in their faith and develop a deeper relationship with God. You have the potential to touch lives forever as you prepare students for a responsible role in society and the Church.

An important question for Catholic school educators to ask themselves each day is: **"Am I a teacher in a Catholic school or a Catholic school teacher?"** There is a difference between the two. A teacher in a Catholic school sees their work as simply a job, or perhaps they view themselves as a facilitator of curriculum. A Catholic school teacher sees their work very differently. A Catholic school teacher believes their work is a calling, a vocation, a ministerial opportunity to serve as an ambassador of Jesus and the Catholic Church. As such, the teacher understands the need to live their faith and support the teachings of the Church in all interactions with students and parents.

The role of the Catholic school teacher has expanded and become more challenging and complex. More than ever before there is a great need and a responsibility to serve as a role model for students. When you teach the truths of the Gospel, your students expect you to act accordingly. Students look to you to live Gospel values. They will not tolerate hypocrisy and double standards. They expect the adults in their lives to be positive role models in their words, actions and appearance.

Your appearance, words, and behavior influence the way students, parents/guardians, and your colleagues perceive you. It is essential that they see you as a consummate professional in all that you do at all times!

Test Your Professional Conduct IQ

Directions: Read the following statements carefully and answer **TRUE** or **FALSE.** Discuss your responses with your colleagues. (The answers can be found at the end of the book.)

As a professional Catholic school educator, it is important to:

1. Dress like my students so that they can relate better to me.
2. Avoid texting and using other electronic messaging during professional meetings and while performing supervisory duties.
3. Formally introduce myself to parents/guardians so that I can establish a professional relationship.
4. Return calls to parents/guardians at my convenience.
5. Refrain from discussions regarding my personal life with my students.
6. Apply rules of grammar to all school-related communications.
7. Begin and/or end professional meetings with prayer.
8. Have different expectations of dress and behavior for my students than for myself.
9. Seek to create a spirit of collaboration with parents/guardians.
10. Recognize that facial expression, posture and tone communicate a message.
11. Become "friends" with students or parents/guardians on personal social networking sites.
12. Use good judgment when it is necessary to be alone with a student.

Professional Appearance

"As you dress so shall you be perceived, as you are perceived so shall you be judged."
—Harry Wong

The ABCs of Appropriate Dress for the Catholic School Educator

Dress to impress is the rule! When you arrived at the interview for your teaching position, more than likely you made sure your appearance was impeccable, including fresh-pressed clothing, clean fingernails and hands, and polished shoes. Along with your credentials, you realized your appearance was equally important in making a good impression on the interviewer. You dressed to impress that day. Now that you have the position, why should any other day be different? Keep dressing to

impress. It is what professionals do!

Each staff member in a Catholic school has the potential to make an impact on students. All Catholic school educators have a responsibility to serve as role models for students by dressing in a professional manner. Staff attire should rarely contradict anything that is prohibited for student attire. To do so creates a confusing double standard for students and diminishes the credibility and authority of the professional staff. Inappropriate dress also sends a nonverbal message to parents/guardians and students that "what I am doing here is really not that important" or "the people for whom I am doing it are really not that important."

Parents/guardians who choose to send their children to a Catholic school value the high standards and expectations set for students. They expect teachers to consistently serve as role models for their children and to help them in the formation of positive lifelong habits. The professional attire of the teacher affects the work, attitudes and behavior of the students. A professional image also creates an atmosphere of respect and builds the staff's credibility. The professional "uniform" of teachers conveys an attitude of love and respect for the children. Remember, as a teacher you represent the profession, the school, your faith and yourself.

Here are some guidelines for Catholic school personnel that may help to create a professional appearance:

BUSINESS ATTIRE

Men:
- Collared shirts
- Dress slacks
- Sweaters or cardigans
- Jackets, blazers, suits (optional)
- Ties (not required but suggested)
- Dress shoes

Women:
- Business suits or dresses
- Pant suits
- Skirts, dress slacks
- Blouses, blazers, sweaters
- Dress shoes

BUSINESS CASUAL ATTIRE FOR MEN AND WOMEN
(when students are not present)

- Collared shirts or blouses
- Slacks, Dockers, chinos, khakis, jeans (that fit and look neat and clean)
- Polo shirts
- Turtlenecks or sweaters
- Sweaters or cardigans
- Casual shoes

UNACCEPTABLE ATTIRE FOR EITHER BUSINESS OR BUSINESS CASUAL ATTIRE

- Athletic wear, jumpsuits, shorts, cargo pants
- T-shirts, tank tops, halter tops, spaghetti straps
- Very short skirts or dresses
- Leggings, sweatpants, jogging suits, yoga pants
- Athletic shoes, hiking boots, clogs, "UGG"-style boots and beach type sandals such as flip-flops. (Inappropriate footwear, such as flip-flops, pose a safety threat, especially in a school emergency.)
- Sheer, revealing or tight-fitting clothing, immodest necklines
- Tattered clothing, apparel with slogans
- Sunglasses indoors

A general rule to follow—if you would wear it to the beach or a barbecue, don't wear it to school!

OTHER EXPECTATIONS FOR PROFESSIONAL APPEARANCE

- Facial and body piercings are not appropriate in a school setting
- Tattoos are to be covered at all times
- Accessories should be simple, in good taste, and not excessive
- Colognes and fragrances should be avoided or used in moderation (many people have allergies to these)
- Select apparel, jewelry and hairstyles that are in good taste and do not detract from your professional appearance

SPECIAL CONSIDERATIONS FOR STAFF ATTIRE

- The attire for staff in positions such as physical education, pre-school, before and after school care may call for a more relaxed attire due to the nature of their work.
- Outdoor field trips, picnics, dress-down days, walkathons, fun fairs, etc., may call for a more relaxed dress code for the staff; however, good judgment should be used in choosing appropriate casual attire.
- In all cases, follow the expectations for attire set by the local school administrator.

Professional Meetings

"...for where two or more are gathered in my name, I am there in the middle of them..."
—MATTHEW 18:19-20

Preparation and Participation

Expectations and Behavior of Teachers at Professional Meetings

Faculty and other professional development meetings are integral to the ongoing personal growth of those serving in Catholic schools. As professionals, all staff members have a responsibility to participate each time they attend a meeting. When all attendees participate fully, the goals and objectives of the school's mission and philosophy are successfully achieved. Therefore, Catholic educators should be mindful that their actions set the tone of the meeting. A positive, professional attitude will enable the school faculty to grow as a faith-filled learning community. Here are some guidelines that can help educators learn the importance of acting professionally while attending meetings.

Climate and Culture

■ Professional meetings in Catholic school settings should begin and end with respectful prayer.

■ Teachers may be asked to share the responsibility of preparing and leading prayer. Whenever possible, signs and symbols of the faith should be present in order to create an environment that enables participants to engage in prayer in meaningful ways. Seasons of the Church year should be incorporated in the prayer.

Meeting Etiquette

■ Attendance at meetings is a required part of the workday and an important part of your ministry. Avoid asking for personal time on these days. Also, arrive at professional meetings on time and stay until the conclusion.

■ If there is a social gathering prior to or following the meeting, teachers should consider these gatherings a required part of the meeting.

■ Study the agenda and materials beforehand. Come prepared to engage in discussion and offer input as needed.

■ While it is natural to want to sit with teachers in your grade level or subject area, consider sitting with other teachers which gives you the opportunity to get to know others and strengthen relationships throughout the school. This is also a good way to create a positive work environment.

■ Participate fully in the meeting by being an active listener. It is never appropriate to engage in tasks such as grading student work, perusing irrelevant reading materials, checking your cell phone, tablet or other device, or conducting personal business during the meeting. Your full attention and participation are essential to your personal growth as a Catholic educator.

■ It is not professional to carry on "sidebar" conversations or make inappropriate comments during a meeting. This is a distraction to the presenter(s) and others around you and demonstrates an attitude of disrespect.

- Be organized. Come prepared to take notes on items of importance and keep a file of your notes along with agendas and minutes from previous meetings.
- Remember to silence your cell phone or any other electronic device prior to the start of the meeting. **Never** text message or check emails during a meeting.

Interpersonal Skills

- Be a good listener by allowing others time to share their thoughts and ideas without interruption.
- When asked for input, be objective and see things from multiple points of view. Decisions should be the result of open and honest communication and reflective listening. Remember that like you, those present are working toward making decisions that are in the best interest of the students and the school.
- Use tact when dealing with difficult participants or controversial issues.
- Always compliment and thank colleagues for their contributions to or service on committees.
- Remember that you have a responsibility to uphold the decisions reached by consensus of the faculty and always follow the directives of the principal.
- When attending a professional meeting, display the same behavior that you expect of the students in your classroom. To do otherwise is a double standard and diminishes your professionalism and credibility.

Developing Effective Communication Skills

*"Teachers, I believe are the most responsible
and important members of society, because their
professional efforts affect the fate of the earth."*
—HELEN CALDICOTT

Effective Catholic school teachers understand the importance of weaving together both the art and science of communication. The art of communication involves creating an environment that builds and enhances trust, respect and openness within the faith-centered community. The science of communication encourages the development of skills and strategies that promote positive communication through the use of meaningful feedback, empathetic listening and

collaboration. Whether you are greeting students as they enter your classroom, welcoming parents to a conference, creating a home/school communication, or resolving a conflict, effective communication promotes the mission of the Catholic school and provides an ideal opportunity in which to teach the Gospel message.

General Guidelines for Effective Communication in the Catholic School

- Focus on supporting the mission and philosophy of the Catholic school through your words and actions.
- Practice engaged, empathetic listening.
- Practice collaboration with your colleagues, the administration and parents.
- Speak truthfully, with kindness and respect.
- Always support what is best for student learning.
- Be accountable by providing feedback and thorough follow-up.
- Invite questions and genuinely value the opinions of others.
- Keep parents, administrators and students informed.
- Maintain an atmosphere of respect and trust supported by shared values.

Verbal and Non-Verbal Communication

Follow formal grammatical rules in your professional speech. Initiate positive conversations and dialogue that build meaningful relationships. Your professional image is directly linked to the words you choose and the way in which you express yourself.

- Strive to develop a vocabulary that is both direct and concise.
- Speak with confidence and enthusiasm.
- Avoid the use of slang, off-color words, and trendy expressions with adults and your students.
- Take note of pronunciation and grammar rules.

- Use appropriate volume and tone when you are speaking to an individual or a group.
- Make eye contact, extend a firm handshake, and smile warmly.
- Recognize that your facial expression, posture and gestures send messages to the listener.
- Convey friendliness and a positive attitude in words and actions.

Written Communication

- Follow formal grammatical rules in all written forms of communication including newsletters, messages, email, notes to parents and business correspondence.
- Be sure to check spelling to verify accuracy.
- Before sending school communications, have an administrator or colleague proofread them.
- Remain objective in tone and content. If a sensitive or controversial subject needs to be addressed in writing to parents or colleagues, avoid being reactionary by allowing yourself adequate "wait time" before responding.
- Avoid ambiguity. Be concise, clear and specific, while always keeping the mission of the Catholic school in focus.

Social Media Guidelines

"Let your speech always be gracious, seasoned with salt, so that you may know how to answer each person."
—COLOSSIANS 4:6

Internet Etiquette

- Your emails are professional correspondence.
- Always convey a polite and pleasant tone in emails and other electronic communication.
- As a professional courtesy, follow standard writing guidelines; text message language, abbreviations, intentional misspellings, and emoticons should be avoided.
- Use the "reply," "reply all" and "forward" functions carefully and appropriately.
- Electronic communication can never replace personal contact, especially when dealing with sensitive or complex situations.
- All Internet use at school must pertain to school-related issues, topics and needs.

- As a protection to you, keep a folder of emails sent to and received from parents/guardians.

Internet Style

- Be aware that the recipient of an email does not have the benefit of voice or vocal expression when interpreting a message.
- Address the recipient appropriately and put your name and position on all emails. Remember that you are communicating with a person, not another computer.
- Use bold, italic or all capital letters sparingly and never to emphasize a thought or a personal emotion.
- Use the automated spelling/grammar check to ensure that your text is error free.
- Copy the administrator on all emails sent to parents/guardians. Similarly, copy the administrator (selectively) when sending emails to professional colleagues.

Appropriate Use of Technology

- Know that all messages and information you send and receive are public and permanent.
- As an educator, you are always "on duty." Keep in mind that electronic messages are neither anonymous nor private. They can be tracked, forwarded, misdirected and live forever on the Internet.
- Do not use social media sites to post negative comments or statements about your students, their parents/guardians, your colleagues, your immediate supervisor, or the school system in which you are employed.
- While social media sites can be a wonderful way to connect with family and friends, by the nature of their position, educators must exercise caution in terms of what is posted. Be mindful that anything can be shared beyond one's group of Internet "friends." Information and photos can be easily copied and transferred to anyone.
- Be prudent on personal social media sites. One cannot make disparaging comments about colleagues and supervisors and not expect to jeopardize their – or your – position.

- Sharing personal email accounts and/or social networking sites with students and parents/guardians is never appropriate. Only the school email address or school social media site should be shared.
- Texting, instant messaging and other informal methods of electronic communication with parents and students should be avoided.
- Use your school assigned email account and your school computer for professional purposes only. It is not appropriate to engage in personal use of electronic communication during the school day, (e.g., cell phone conversations, Internet shopping, visiting personal Internet sites). As a professional, your time at school should be spent giving students undivided attention during class time and on planning instruction during planning periods.
- As a rule, cell phones should be turned off during class time.
- In the event of a personal emergency, use cell phones in designated school areas removed from the classroom setting and ensure that students are adequately supervised as needed.
- In the event of a school-related emergency, cell phones may be used to communicate the situation to the administration or local authorities.
- Become familiar with your local school policy on photo permission and media release. In general, it is not acceptable to post photos or videos of students on public sites without written parental permission.

Maintaining Professional Boundaries

As professional Catholic educators, it is essential that teachers maintain a positive, appropriate relationship with students and their families. Though we love and have a great fondness for our students, at the same time we must acknowledge that we are not their friends. In addition, teachers are legally held to a high standard of care to protect their students. Therefore, professional Catholic educators should avoid:

- Being alone with a student out of the view of others and without informing a supervisor or colleague.
- Befriending students on social networking sites and social networking with students for non-educational purposes.
- Using sarcasm, slang, foul language, inappropriate humor, ridicule, labeling and name calling.
- Discussing highly personal matters with students (e.g., your relationships, finances, outside activities).

Additional Communication and General Etiquette Tips

"Be kind and merciful, let no one come to you without coming away better and happier."
—MOTHER TERESA

Informal Meetings and Greetings

Throughout the school year, Catholic school educators will interact with parents and other visitors during the school day, after school hours, and at various school and community events. These are ideal settings in which to develop positive relationships and enhance the public relations efforts of your school. Teachers are important "ambassadors" in promoting the values, mission and goals of the school. They play a vital role in sharing the good news of their Catholic school community. The effective Catholic school educator smiles warmly, greets others, and genuinely welcomes students, parents, colleagues and visitors. You are part of a faith community that can only be built on trust, respect and meaningful relationships.

Guidelines for Professional Meeting and Greeting

When greeting parents or visitors, be a model "ambassador" for your school by following these rules of professional etiquette:

- Introduce yourself formally as Mr., Mrs., Ms., Miss, Father, Brother, Sister or other formal title, and clarify your role in the school.
- When appropriate, offer a firm, warm handshake while making eye contact with the person.
- Call them by title throughout the conversation.
- Ask them something about their children, particularly when they are new to the school.
- Make an effort to help them feel relaxed and welcomed in the school.
- Conclude by expressing how pleased you are to have had an opportunity to meet them.

General Etiquette Tips

Attendance and Punctuality

Generally, the faculty handbook and teacher contract outline the hours teachers are expected to be present in the building. Abide by the attendance requirements set by the administration. When it is necessary to be absent or late, or to leave early, always seek the approval of the principal. Most administrators will understand, particularly in extenuating circumstances such as family illnesses and other emergencies. Keep in mind that in your absence, the administrator has the responsibility to provide supervision for the students assigned to you. Timely communication of your need to be absent or away from the school enables the administrator to secure an adequate substitute.

Work Effectiveness

Always use work time efficiently, particularly when using technology. When you have planning time away from the students, make a strong effort to engage in appropriate work-related tasks. Meet the deadlines for responding to the administrator's requests.

Relating to the Administrator

Always be mindful of the fact that, in most cases, the principal is your boss and immediate supervisor. Most administrators work very hard at strengthening relationships with their staffs. Follow the principal's directives and support his/her decisions, even the unpopular ones. When you disagree with your principal on an issue, express your disagreement honestly, respectfully and privately.

Learn the principal's preferred method of communication such as email, phone call, office drop in or scheduled meeting. Respect the preferred method.

Always give the principal a "heads up" about an upcoming issue involving students and parents/guardians.

Relating to Parents/Guardians

Parents are the primary educators of their children. It is important to recognize them as partners in the educational process. Treat all parents/guardians with empathy, respect, integrity and compassion. When problems arise with student performance or behavior (and they will), make an effort to understand the student's home situation. Realize that this can greatly impact the child's academic performance and social behavior at school. Listen attentively to the needs and opinions of the parent/guardian and be sensitive to their limitations. See if you can come up with ways of making the situation with their child less burdensome for them.

Parents appreciate knowing that their children are loved. Remember to say something kind about their child. When you recognize the personal gifts of the child, it lets the parent know that you truly care about helping their child succeed. Never deliver bad news about their child via email. Ask for a face-to-face or phone meeting to discuss major issues and concerns. Always show parents the respect they expect and deserve from a Catholic school professional and hopefully, you will receive the same in return!

Relating to Colleagues

One of the best models of positive relationships for students is how staff interacts with one another. When conversing with other teachers in front of students, use appropriate language, speak respectfully and only engage in conversation about topics regarding the school. Remember to use appropriate titles when addressing your colleagues in front of the children.

Avoid cliques among the faculty. Never allow age, gender or position to separate you from working together to fulfill the mission and goals of the school. If we want our students to be accepting of others, we must practice the same example of behavior that we try to teach them.

Keep conversations about students and their families respectful and appropriate. Gossip about your students and their parents is hurtful and labels them. It also sets students up for failure as they progress through their school years. Do not allow the faculty room to become the place for negative conversations about your students and their families.

Keep email communication among colleagues professional and work related. Avoid sending emails that are personal and/or sensitive in nature, particularly during the school day. Not everyone enjoys receiving the off-color jokes and stories that are sometimes circulated.

Epilogue

THERE IS NO QUESTION that professionalism for Catholic educators includes appropriate dress and appearance, effective communication and general rules of etiquette. However, it is essential to remember that professionalism extends beyond outward appearance and social behavior to the core of your being. The key to becoming a consummate professional is an inner disposition of faith, prayer, a positive attitude and a genuine love for the ministry of Catholic school education.

First and foremost, Catholic school educators must be people of prayer who value deepening their relationship with God. They incorporate Gospel values into every aspect of their lives and relationships and generously share their gifts with others. They reflect on their own behaviors and attitudes, admit their mistakes, and seek to become better persons and educators by learning from them. Professional Catholic school educators value the God-given gifts and talents of others and respond with respect to every person at all times.

That is the heart of being a professional Catholic school educator. That is what differentiates a teacher in a Catholic school from a *Catholic school teacher!*

Answers to the "Test Your Professional Conduct IQ" Assessment

1.   **False**

2.   **True**

3.   **True**

4.   **False**

5.   **True**

6.   **True**

7.   **True**

8.   **False**

9.   **True**

10.   **True**

11.   **False**

12.   **True**

Reflection for a Catholic School Teacher:

A Ministry or a Job?

❖ Some people have a job in the Church.

❖ Others invite themselves into a ministry.

❖ What is the difference, you ask?

❖ If you are doing it just because no one else will, it is a job.

❖ If you are doing it to serve the Lord, it's a ministry.

❖ If you quit because someone else criticized you, it is a job.

❖ If you keep on serving, it is a ministry.

❖ If you will do it as long as it does not interfere with your other activities, it is a job.

❖ If you are committed to staying even if it means letting go of other things, it is a ministry.

❖ If you quit because no one thanked you or praised you, it is a job.

❖ If you stick with it even though no one recognized your efforts, it is a ministry.

❖ It is hard to get excited about a job.

❖ It is almost impossible not to get excited about a ministry.

❖ If your concern is success, it is a job.

❖ If your concern is faithfulness and service, it is a ministry.

❖ If God calls you to a ministry, do not treat it like a job!

About the Author

Sal Guccione has been a Catholic school educator for 40 years. He has served as a teacher, school principal and an assistant superintendent for the Archdiocese of Chicago. Sal also served as the Great Lakes States representative for the NCEA Elementary Schools Department Executive Committee from 2005 until 2013. At present, he serves as an independent Catholic school consultant presenting workshops and providing consultation on a variety of school matters. He currently resides in Chicago.

Acknowledgments

Special recognition and gratitude to the following Catholic school professionals for volunteering their time to edit and share their expertise in the development of this publication.

Dr. Amy Mills
Principal, Our Lady of Perpetual Help School, Glenview, Illinois

Mr. Adam Dufault
Principal, St, Catherine Labouré School, Glenview, Illinois

Mr. Roy Hecker
Principal, Pope John XXIII School, Evanston, Illinois

Notes

Notes